LOVING EVERY MOMENT

LOVING EVERY MOMENT

DAVID STIRLING
with Uranda Stirling

LOVING EVERY MOMENT BOOKS
in association with
POLAIR PUBLISHING
LONDON

First Published 2011 by
Loving Every Moment Books
in association with Polair Publishing

© Copyright David Stirling,
Uranda Stirling, 2011

**British Library Cataloguing
in Publication Data**
*A catalogue record for this book is
available from the British Library*

ISBN 978-1-905398-23-2

*Editorial, typesetting and design services by
Colum Hayward Consultancy
Printed in Great Britain by Cambridge University Press*

CONTENTS

Dedication · 8
Foreword by Richard Lang · 9

Introduction · 11
Using the Book · 17
Some of the things Jesus and the
Apostles say about Love · 19
A Note about Some of the Terms Used · 23
Some Final Thoughts · 25
And Last of All · 25

Chapter 1 · The Logical Mind – or the Heart? · 27
What we Really Are · 29
Love and Light · 35
An Example in Action of 'Loving Every Moment' · 37
Another Story · 39
Affirmations · 41

Chapter 2 · What is Love? · 45
Real Love · 46
Another Example · 47
Summary · 49

Loving Natural Things · 50
Some Thoughts · 51
Further Ideas to Meditate on · 52
Affirmations · 53

Chapter 3 · Methods of Loving · 57
An Experience of Loving · 57
Methods of Loving · 62
Thoughts to Explore · 63
Global Loving · 63
The Love Blanket · 65
Another Way of Applying Love · 66
Affirmations · 68

Chapter 4 · Love Your Self · 73
Going up the Ladder · 75
A Practice using Frequency · 76
An Exercise to do Now · 77
Another Story · 78
More you Can Work on · 79
A Story about Ego · 81
Love your Humanity, as well as your Divinity · 82
Our Forgiving Nature · 83
Our Thoughts are Where All Things Begin · 84
Affirmations · 86

Chapter 5 · Loving Relationships · 93
Emotions · 94
Some More Thoughts · 96
Loving Fears · 99
Love All your Negative and Positive Emotions · 100
Affirmations · 100

Chapter · Utilizing the Daily Love List · 105
A Sample 'Daily Love List' 110

Chapter 7 · Loving Every Moment · 119
Love–Light · 121
Let's Sum up · 122
And Lastly · 123

Index of Individual Skills and Techniques · 124

Dedication by David Stirling

*I have enjoyed the most wonderful
support in so many ways from my best
friend, wife, and co-author, Uranda, while
we went through the processes of life over the
past twenty-four years and more. Those processes
both enabled us and gave us the need to practise
'loving everyone, and everything'.
Without Uranda tirelessly providing wisdom
during tension-filled business years and other
exigencies, and without her untiring caring and
her healings – which kept me alive through a
time of utter debilitation of health, this book
would never have been written.
The uncountable numbers of deep
discussions we enjoyed, and the sharing of
each other's spiritual understandings, contributed
immensely to the actual practices presented herein.
In every sense Uranda is the co-author of this book.
Thank you, my dear Uranda, I dedicate
Loving Every Moment
to you.
David*

FOREWORD
by Richard Lang, author of
Seeing who You Really Are: a Modern Guide to your True Identity

I FIRST met David Stirling several years ago. David has been aware of his true self for many years and contacted me after reading my book on this subject. We became friends – friends who share a wonderful, open secret. Anyone who sees their true self expresses this open secret in their own way, but at the heart of any expression of this truth will be love, for your true self *is* love.

In this short book David speaks about the truth and power of love. He shows you how it can work in your life, and gives you practical ways of applying this love in any and every situation.

As David makes clear, you don't have to understand how it works for it to work. But David doesn't just speak about love, he takes you by the hand and, practising what he preaches, enfolds you in love.

Through David's words comes the love he speaks about – wise, patient, healing, unconditional…

Read this book, awaken to your true self which is love, practise the art of loving, and receive the countless blessings that flow from this awareness.

Richard Lang
June 2011

INTRODUCTION

AS A CHILD, I was surrounded by love. My parents had emigrated to Canada from Scotland in 1929 right in the middle of the great depression. They fell in love in Scotland, came to Canada and married, and I was born in 1932. My brother followed five years later. Mom and Dad both came from large families, but they were the only ones that had the nerve to embark on such a great adventure. No other family members ever migrated anywhere.

As well as loving each other, and my brother and I, they loved everyone and everything around them – and Mom and Dad were loved by everyone who knew them. Mom and Dad gave my brother and I a secure and solid home life and taught us, by example, their strong values of love, respect, and compassion for others, and the fact that everything good in life came from God our Father–Mother.

From our own Mom and Dad we also learned 'thankfulness to God' for all our many blessings, and to express our thankfulness every day.

Even though tough depression times were with them from the day they landed in Canada, my father got a job right away, and was never a day out of work. My dear mother also worked. Both parents were honest, diligent workers, and their employers always appreciated them.

We had a modest home, but it was filled to overflowing with love, and we never wanted for any of the necessities of life.

It was from this loving environment that I began to learn the difference between human love and divine love, and it was from understanding that difference that I came to learn how I could simply and easily apply 'the power of love'. Just what this is, is what will be disclosed to you in the chapters that follow. Through it, I believe that you will learn to apply the power of love, and moreover that you will love applying it!

In this book I have set forth my practices and affirmations, and some of my subsequent experiences, as well as the experiences of others, in applying the power of love. Once discovered, this secret gave me, and continues to give me, peace and happiness in my life.

All experience the power of love continuously every day, but sadly most are unaware of doing so, even though the power of love is the mainstay of all life on both sides of the veil. Without it, there could be no life at all.

Over many years, the great truths of the power of love have been misunderstood or ignored by most. However, we now live in a time when more people than ever before understand, or have a feel for it, or have a sincere desire to do so. The power of love is very readily utilized, and can be easily accessed just by applying it.

When you apply divine love by the simple methods presented in these pages, I believe you will reap the enormous benefits that God our Father intends for us all.

Divine love is the most powerful energy in the Cosmos – bar none.

★

What you are about to undertake is an experiential process, not a 'learning' of something new. You already know it all – but have forgotten it temporarily, and just need to rediscover it.

Quite often, students of the truth read many

books and some go to numerous seminars. These activities are in themselves perfectly OK, but none of them will 'enlighten' you, unless you seriously *apply* what you read or hear.

Applying does not just mean reading and re-reading: it means really, continuously, utilizing and applying what you discover.

Sooner or later we all must apply that which we inherently have within us – in order to arrive back at the truth. You most certainly will enjoy the results of applying 'loving'.

The simple, but so powerful application of 'loving' – should be, indeed *must* be, practised from the heart. 'The heart' means your reality – conscious pure awareness, the totally 'detached' knower, witness, seer of all things and all thoughts. So set your 'logical' mind aside, during your sojourn here, and be in your heart. You are in your heart every time you feel any love at all for someone or something – a small baby, a pet, the beauties of nature; or for someone who has shown courage or inner strength.

It is not necessary for you to understand the 'hows' of its workings, any more than you need understand the technology that illuminates a light bulb when you switch it on. Just enjoy it the same way as you enjoy the benefit of the light bulb. Do it *consciously*.

INTRODUCTION

Many sages and great teachers over the centuries have advised humankind to 'go within' – which I believe means to go into the heart.

Very few of them tell you how to get there. However, if we have followed the words of Jesus, the Christ, we already have been reliably assured that none shall be left behind.

We will all get there, even without utilizing the applications set forth here and in a few other places, but it will take a lot longer to do so, and quite possibly much more suffering will need be endured. So why not do it now?

★

Here in this book is a simple method for consciously letting go, and 'loving everything'.

It is very important that you just try applying what is on these pages without analyzing the words used to describe the method, and instead experience the magnificent peace and bliss that practising the techniques will raise within you – for the power to do so is already within you, in the Christ Light, the presence of God our Father. It is within everyone's heart.

I have been on the 'path', so to speak, for at least forty years of this life, and have read many books, and attended some seminars and other events, and

I have had the privilege of meeting a few great masters, but, very, very few tell you how to practise their message, and even fewer give you the actual practice format.

I believe that what is presented here is straightforward and easily understood, and will show you the way to 'get out of your mind' and 'get into your heart'.

So what is the answer if you want continuously to enjoy peace and wellbeing?

You have the answer right in your hands:

> **Apply Love!**

You can do it all yourself, because your own guru is already within your heart, and is ready to show you the way. He is patiently waiting for your knock on his door, and he will take your hand, and walk with you every step of the way home.

And you will be going home in all reality. You came from the bliss that you long for, and are going back to – but you have just forgotten it.

What you will rediscover here in these practices will help you remember your reality, and your guru.

Enjoy your practices, and welcome home!

INTRODUCTION

Today is a gift, from God our Father,
That is why it is called 'the present'!

USING THE BOOK

You will see throughout these pages the letters 'H&N', H&N . These simply mean 'Here and Now' – where your consciousness needs to be!

You will also see 'TYG', TYG , as on the previous page. It stands for 'Thank You God'.

I have always lived with the premise that I must express my gratitude by saying 'thank you' to whoever is providing me any kindness, or goods or services in any manner, small or large. And I certainly believe that God our Father not only provides us our very life, but every breath we breathe, along with everything else we need throughout our lives. I also believe that one can never be 'too' thankful. I am immensely grateful for all the blessings He bestows upon us all. This is why the 'TYG' has been placed at all the appropriate places. Use it as much as you like!

I like to have quite a dialogue with myself when I am practising loving, so that I stand outside of the familiar personality, as it were. Thus when you meet 'David' in the text, it's me talking to me!

Any place you see x3 , 'x 3', after a statement

(usually an affirmation), it means to repeat it three times. Please do this if you want the practice to have the greatest effect.

The best way to benefit from reading this book is to start from the beginning, and proceed through the book chapter by chapter to the end. Do not jump around, certainly not on your first reading. After that, you can go to various pages that have particular interest for you, but with the first reading I heartily recommend you do as recommended here.

Read each chapter, one after another, thoroughly, paragraph by paragraph, missing nothing. Wherever you are given an instruction, do exactly as recommended. There are pages provided for notes if you like to write things down.

You will achieve much more if you read this book, especially its affirmations, aloud. The spoken word is much more powerful than the silent word, so please take advantage of this. Read aloud! Repeat the affirmations aloud, and with strength of enthusiasm.

I have also included, at the end of each chapter, some words headed 'Affirmation Chant'. This above all is best read aloud, or even chanted, as a practice in itself.

Now some words which show how authentic is the practice in this book.

INTRODUCTION

Some of the things Jesus and the Apostles say about love

You can quite usefully say these to yourself, as affirmations or as ways of guiding your thoughts into the heart. I have used all sorts of versions of the Bible in this book, so some will be less familiar and others will feel very reassuring.

John 13:34
A new commandment I give unto you, That ye love one another; as I have loved you, that ye also love one another. TYG

John 13:35
By this shall all men know that ye are my disciples, if ye have love one to another. TYG

John 15:12
This is my commandment, That ye love one another, as I have loved you. TYG

John 15:17
These things I command you, that ye love one another. TYG

Galatians 5:13
For, brethren, ye have been called unto liberty; only use not liberty for an occasion to the flesh, but by love serve one another. TYG

1 Thessalonians 4:9
But as touching brotherly love ye need not that I write unto you: for ye yourselves are taught of God to love one another. TYG

Peter 1:22
Seeing ye have purified your souls in obeying the truth through the Spirit unto unfeigned love of the brethren, see that ye love one another with a pure heart fervently. TYG

1 Peter 3:8
Finally, be ye all of one mind, having compassion one of another, love as brethren, be pitiful, be courteous. TYG

1 John 3:11*
For this is the message that ye heard from the beginning, that we shouldlove one another. TYG

*I have found that all of 1 John 3 is worth reading)

1 Corinthians 13
Love is the greatest!

13:1 If I could speak all the languages of earth and of angels, but didn't love others, I would be a noisy gong or a clanging cymbal. TYG

13:2 If I had the gift of prophecy, and if I understood all of God's secret plans and possessed all knowledge, and if I had such faith that I could move mountains, but didn't love others, I would be nothing. TYG

13:3 If I gave everything I have to the poor – and even sacrificed my body, I could boast about it; but if I didn't love others, I would have gained nothing. TYG

13:4 Love is patient and kind. TYG

13:5 Love is not jealous or boastful or proud or rude. It does not demand its own way. It is not irritable, and it keeps no record of being wronged. TYG

13:6 It does not rejoice about injustice but rejoices whenever the truth wins out. TYG

13:7 Love never gives up, never loses faith, is always hopeful, and endures through every circumstance. TYG

13:8 Prophecy and speaking in unknown languages and special knowledge will become useless. But love will last forever! TYG

13:13 Three things will last forever – faith – hope – and love – and the greatest of these is love. TYG

Mathew 21:22
Therefore I say unto you, what thing soever ye desire, when ye pray, believe that ye receive them, and ye shall have them'. TYG

Mark 11:24
And all things, whatsoever ye shall ask in prayer, believing, ye shall receive. TYG

A Prayer
Dear God, Show me the way … to love … to love all my tests this day. TYG

INTRODUCTION

A Note about Some of the Terms Used

There are very few words in the book that need explaining, but I'd particularly like to mention the terms 'higher self' and 'lower self'. The 'lower self' will be very familiar to you – it's the one that you tend to run up against all the time, that tells you your limitations and holds your fears. The 'higher self' is the one that comes into play when you overcome your fears – decide to trust someone or something, not fear it – and so become part of the larger, higher community of life and not a little, separate unit. You'll know this feeling, however infrequently you get it, because it feels so good. It may come all of a sudden when you hear beautiful music or see something lovely like the sun setting over the sea. You stand in your own self-awareness and don't feel limited – not because of ego but because you don't feel separate from life any longer. That's what 'the higher self' means. Another way you might look at it in a Christian context is that the higher self is when you feel full of the light of Christ. You'll find I sometimes refer to 'the Christ light in me'.

You'll quickly understand, indeed you will know it from my opening remarks, that I was brought up in a strong Christian tradition, yet I believe that the path of 'Loving Every Moment' is open to all. If you belong to another tradition you will just have to change my vocabulary slightly – the overall idea still stands. I like to think of Christianity as strongly connecting with all the other great religions. You will find Buddha quoted in this book, therefore, and the concept of the 'etheric body', which I use, as well as the idea of the higher and lower self, comes originally from Hinduism – though it is very popular in the New Age movement today. Hinduism has a word for the etheric body that literally means the 'breath body' – a body which needs only the nourishment of physical breath for its existence. I also use the terms 'mental body' and 'emotional body' alongside the 'physical body'. All this means is that just as we have a physical body to take on what we need to do on the physical plane, so there is a body constructed by our thoughts and another constructed by our emotions, and so on. You feel pain in the emotional body as well as the physical, and the mental body is capable of great thoughts as well as some pretty limited ones. Apply love to them, and they heal, each in their own way. I also refer to my 'global body' – this is the whole body, containing all the parts, and more than the sum of them.

Some final thoughts

1. Being the presence of love is easier than you might think. One need never judge, but only love … that is, love everything, just the way it is.
2. You are your 'higher self' (spirit, awareness, inner light). Once you accept this truth, then there is really nothing else with which you can identify except this. It is only the light within you, the centre that is God, that is eternal and unchanging.
3. You will become aware that all the other identities (the 'lower self', made up of the etheric, physical, mental, and emotional bodies or layers) are transient – they are forever changing and dissolve in the end.

And Last of All

This is a small but very powerful book. The power set forth in this book is immediately available to you – if you apply it properly.

Love–Light is the most powerful energy in the universe.

Apply what you read here, and you will experience the great life that God our Father intended that we all enjoy.

God bless you….

NOTES

CHAPTER ONE

THE LOGICAL MIND – OR THE HEART?

I WAS most fortunate, as I have said, in being able to enjoy a very loving mother and father. They not only loved my brother and I very much, but they loved pretty well everyone, and all of life in general. They weren't rich materially, but they were very rich in love, the only thing that really matters.

My parents weren't regular churchgoers, but they were very spiritually-minded and consciously and continuously lived with God's presence. For example, my father never proposed anything without prefacing it with the phrase, 'With the will of God…'.

They sent my brother and me to Sunday School, for which I am eternally grateful. I also enjoyed the daily bible reading and prayers at regular school, which took place in every classroom in those days, first thing in the morning, prior to lessons beginning.

Given that I lived with two very loving parents, who were constantly referring to the love of God, and God's will, and my years of attending Sunday school, and my daily bible reading and prayers at public school for eight years, it's not surprising that I grew up realizing – from a very early age – that God loves us all.

I have a strong recollection of a verse in one of the Psalms that, even when I was a little boy, made a big impact on me:

Though I walk through the valley of the shadow of death, I shall fear no evil, for Thou art with me, Thy Rod and Thy staff they comfort me. (Psalm 23)

I have used this wonderful sentence as a prayer during many moments of fear and foreboding throughout my life (and still do), and every time without fail it has brought me the peace of the love of God our Father and Mother.

I also began the practice of talking with God about all manner of things, and I believe this was brought about by my praying this wonderful, powerful prayer. With the help of this prayer, I became, very aware of the great love of God our Father and

His full protection for us all, and of the love of the Mother God. I also came to understand God's wish that we extend this love for us out to all souls everywhere. I believe that God gave us His commandment to do so through His Son, and our dear Master, friend, and brother, Jesus the Christ:

TYG

John 15:17

These things I command you, that ye love one another.

What we Really Are

Here are some of the precepts I think it would help us to realize in order to find the love within us.

- That we are all Spirit (love, light, pure awareness, the heart). H&N TYG
- That we are all children of God. H&N TYG
- That we are all divine as well as human. H&N TYG
- That we all have full access to divine love, anywhere, at any time. H&N TYG
- That we are not this transitory thing, this terminal body/mind. H&N TYG

Now some more thoughts, which may require a little bit of thinking about. As I said, what the mind offers us is transitory and therefore not real. Let's go further and say that mind is illusion, whereas awareness, which we often locate in the heart, is real. Awareness is like our instinctive perception of truth and our innate knowledge of love.

Mind in fact has two principle aspects, and surprisingly they are both equally illusory. They are both ever-changing, and their lifespans vary greatly from milliseconds to years, but they are all purely temporal (passing) in nature.

What I'd like to call invisible mind, the first aspect of mind, is what we most commonly think of as mind. It's invisible from a human physical perspective and is made up of things such as thought and thoughts. However, invisible mind things are very visible to 'awareness', which is the 'reality' that gives life to all aspects of mind. If awareness did not exist, then mind, invisible or visible – could not exist either.

Visible mind – the other principal aspect of mind – is visible from a human physical perspective and is made up of physical-mind 'things' such as our bodies, houses, planets, stars, automobiles – etc., etc. The human body is very much a part of visible mind, as is every other thing that one can see, however temporal they are. Many 'temporal' invisible mind things become visible as they become manifested into 'temporal' visible things. That is to say, thought creates form: it's how we manifest things on the earth.

Heart, in my language, is another word for awareness. There are several words that mean the same as heart or awareness, but these two are the most descriptive and are used the most.

Awareness is 'pure Spirit'. It never changes. It is the Seer, the Knower of all mind things, invisible, and visible – all of which are within it. Awareness is infinite. It exists without 'mind things' but mind cannot exist without awareness.

'Conscious awareness' or heart are always the same, and are not changing or 'temporal' in the way that all aspects of mind are. The Upanishads of ancient India give us this famous phrase:

The mind is the great slayer of the real

This is a great truth!

'The real' is pure awareness, the witness of all. We are *all* pure awareness, the witness of all.

A witness is someone who sees something taking

place, but is not involved with, nor attached in any way to what he or she is witnessing.

The mind is a most wonderful tool that God has provided us with, but we must not let it rule us. The ego is an illusion of the mind that is not equipped to see the truth (heart, pure awareness). Logical mind is great at adding and subtracting and so on, but it is not great at understanding the reality that lies within the heart.

- The mind is within the heart.
- The heart is beyond all mind/thought.
- The heart is pure awareness, the unattached, the witness of all.

When we live predominantly 'in the mind', we suffer greatly, because we are attached to an illusion. We most certainly do suffer, in various ways, when we live in this ego–mind illusion. We suffer in the physical body in many ways, when we are tormented by thoughts, because of living the illusion that we are our ego or our limited physical body. The sense of limitation is the biggest illusion of all.

*

Without a spiritual practice like the one I am describing, a great deal of the time our thoughts are really out of our control and completely get in the way of our heart understanding. Under these circumstances, the mind truly is 'the great slayer of the real'.

To me this timeless statement means that the mind hides reality – reality being pure awareness, the witness, Spirit/love, or the knower/seer of mind (thoughts, things, situations which are finite and ever changing). Awareness is infinite, and beyond mind, and never changes. Mind cannot 'kill' awareness, because awareness is pure Spirit/love, the ultimate ONE reality. On the other hand mind, which 'arises within awareness', is ever coming and going, and its multifarious parts/thoughts/things are finite and, upon their manifestation, are immediately in a process of dissolving back into awareness/love.

Mind certainly has the power to hide awareness from awareness, when awareness is total being, only aware of the activities of the mind. However, you can be free of the mind – and here you will rediscover how to control it. H&N TYG

How do we consciously abide in love?

We can abide in love simply by the practice of loving everyone, and everything – unconditionally! By 'unconditionally' I mean just the way everyone and everything already is. This is exactly how God our Father–Mother loves us all.

It sounds very difficult, you might say – to love everyone and everything. You might ask, for instance:

- 'How can one love women and children being killed in warfare?'
- 'How can one love the fact that many people are starving?'
- 'How can someone love having his/her wallet stolen?'
- 'How can someone love being homeless? or having cancer?'

And you might also ask: 'Why would I want to love these terrible things?'.

These are all good questions for a 'logical' mind, but you will see as this book unfolds, that 'loving' will do the job!

The answer is:

- By loving them, just the way they are, you will immediately achieve a marvellous peace and bliss. TYG
- Resisting or fighting something gives energy to it. In other words 'resisting' actually creates it at its low/negative frequency. It makes the problem worse, in short! TYG
- By loving things, however unpleasant, at the same time as you help the things you are loving, you will rise in vibration and transmute yourself and them towards love, because you stop 'resisting' them. TYG

- Loving a problem – just the way it is – adds no energy to the problem or to whatever you are applying the loving to – and lets it go on its natural way, ultimately to rise in frequency to that of love. TYG

God is Love

1 John 4:16

'And we have known and believed the love that God hath to us.'

Love and Light

We have ample indication all around us that God loves us all: H&N TYG

- He certainly loves us, even when we can't stand ourselves. He must love us, as He still gives us breath, and life – even when we feel unworthy. TYG
- He must love us, as He gives us whatever we ask for. TYG
- He must love us, because we are here. H&N TYG

So, accept that God loves and accepts you – no matter what – just the way you are.

How can we prove this beyond any doubt whatsoever? And ... how can we put this knowledge to the practical use of improving our lives?

We can do that, and more, very simply, and easily.

Let us remember another great truth written in St John's Epistles:

God is love; and he that dwelleth in love, dwelleth in God, and God in him. (1 John 4:16)

These words express with exactness that God is love and if a person abides in love, then God abides in him or her. H&N TYG

Love and light are one and the same. Jesus Christ said, *I and my Father are one* (John 10:30). Therefore ALL of us and God our Father are one. TYG

I and my Father are one is a very powerful statement that you can make to yourself in time of danger, chaos, confusion, accident, illness, or any need. This call will be very successful, as long as you have a strong belief that it cannot fail, and that you understand that you are calling God, our Father. TYG

There is no limit on the number of times you can use it. TYG Every soul can know God intimately and immediately by the practice of 'loving'. God IS love. H&N TYG

An Example in Action of 'Loving Every Moment'

At a meeting one day, I got into a tense situation with a colleague, in which we started to blame each other for the problem we were facing, and our voices were beginning to rise. I saw we were getting out of control, and I would likely lose the friendship of my colleague, so I excused myself for a few minutes and went to the washroom.

There I stated out loud, 'I love this situation just the way it is'. I repeated this statement about six times. I also started to relax a bit.

I then stated that 'I love the tension in this situation just the way it is'. I repeated this statement about six times. I relaxed even more.

I then stated that 'I love Jim (my colleague) just the way he is'. I repeated this statement about six times. I relaxed much more.

I then said out loud, 'I love David (that's me) – just the way I am'. I repeated this statement about six times. Now I was really relaxing – much more again.

I then stated that 'I love David *and* Jim – just the way they are'. I repeated this statement about six times. Now I was really relaxed, and feeling very good indeed. TYG

This whole thing took less than ten minutes.

I then went back to the meeting, where there was now no tension, nor any dispute. Indeed you would think that there never had been one. Jim agreed to my input as if it was his, and I saw no problem with what he had wanted. TYG

Now, to do this is really simple, but one has to set one's 'logical' mind aside, for the moment – and just try loving.

Before I proceed, here are some notes.
- The 'logical' mind cannot achieve loving. It's simply not built to. TYG
- The heart can achieve loving, as it is from the heart (which is the Source of all) that 'loving' comes. TYG
- Loving comes from the heart (the centre of pure awareness or love) by the utilization of our God-given freewill, which is simply beyond the understanding of the 'logical' mind.

So give the 'logical' mind a rest for the moment while we go forward in the heart! TYG

Loving is as simple as breathing. TYG

So, at last, here's the first lesson in 'Loving Every Moment':

> **We just have to love everything
> – just the way everything is!**

Another Story

Recently I had a reunion with a person I had not seen for twenty-two years, and after four or five hours of recalling old times and having dinner, I began to get quite tired. We parted at 9.30 pm, and at 10.00 pm I retired for the night. I was really quite exhausted, which was very unusual for me, and intended to have a deep sleep.

Despite my hopes, I slept very fitfully, waking up every hour or half hour and feeling imbalanced and unwell. I was feeling so poorly, that I was even thinking of calling the doctor.

My intuition told me that old energy had been awoken because of the reunion and it was now being cleared out of my system, for which I was and am very grateful.

At 5.00 am I was still feeling very poorly and in need of sleep, so I played two thirty-minute sleep-assisting tapes on my iPod, which helped me somewhat.

Towards the end of the last tape, my intuition

told me, 'Wrap your body around with love!', which I had forgotten to do. During my 'pain', so to speak, I was concentrating so much on the discomfort I was experiencing that I had forgotten to apply love to the situation.

I then wrapped my physical body with love, and immediately felt positive changes taking place. TYG

I also wrapped my physical body with light, and immediately felt positive changes taking place. TYG

I repeated it several times, and I 'loved myself' as well several times. TYG

I then was back to 'wrapping everything with love or light', and by then I knew that all was well, because all *is* well. TYG

I thought to myself afterwards,

- It's easy to do – to make the mistake of focusing on and thus energizing the problem, and forgetting to 'wrap it with love', or 'wrap it with light'
- We must guard against forgetting to 'wrap everything with love or light', or we bear the consequences by 'experiencing the pain'. TYG

Affirmations

To help myself remember the principle of loving everything as it is, I find it useful to repeat to myself aloud, over and over, statements such as the following.

1. Uncontrolled mind hides my reality. My pure awareness is the loving witness of all. x3 TYG

2. I do not allow my mind to rule me – as it is not equipped to see or know awareness. x3 TYG

3. Whenever I live predominantly 'in the mind' I suffer greatly. x3 TYG

4. I love the truth that God loves us all – just the way we are. x3 TYG

5. I and my Father are One. x3 TYG

6. I know God intimately, and immediately – by my practising the art of 'loving'. x3 TYG

7. I abide in love – simply by practising loving everyone, and everything – just the way they are. x3 TYG

8. Loving is the loving of things, situations, people – just the way they are. x3 TYG

9. I love everyone and everything – just the way they are – and I achieve bliss. x3 TYG

10. I fill everyone and everything with light – just the way they are – and I achieve bliss. x3 TYG

11. I love myself/my awareness – just the way I

am – and I achieve bliss. x3 TYG

12. I love (your name) – just the way (your name) is. x3 TYG

13. I love this physical body – just the way it is. x3 TYG

14. Loving everyone and everything – just the way they are – helps whatever I am loving to rise in vibration and transmute to love. x3 TYG

15. Loving is really simple, but I have to set my 'logical' mind aside, and just focus on my loving. x3 TYG

16. My 'logical' mind cannot achieve loving. x3 TYG

17. I love my 'logical' mind – just the way it is. x3 TYG

18. Only my heart can achieve loving – as it *is* love. x3 TYG

19. Loving comes from my heart by my utilization of my God-given freewill, and it is simply beyond the belief capabilities of my 'logical' mind. x3 TYG

20. Giving loving kindness is as simple as breathing. x3 TYG

21. I love everything – just the way everything it is. x3 TYG

22. I love from the heart. x3 TYG
23. 'I AM That I AM'. 'That' = Awareness, love, Light, Emptiness, God. x3 TYG

AFFIRMATION CHANT
I am loving kindness – in action in me now.
I am loving kindness – to God alone, I bow.
I am loving kindness – in mighty cosmic power.
I am the Light of God – shining every hour.
I am loving kindness – shining like a sun:
I am God's sacred power – freeing everyone. x3 TYG

NOTES

CHAPTER TWO

WHAT IS LOVE?

I MUST tell you a short story that explains perfectly how I learned to love the very thing I found it most difficult to love.

Like many of us, as a child I had always been afraid of the dark. Then one night, lying in bed and still feeling frightened, I decided I really did not want to be afraid of the dark any more.

I simply said, out loud, 'I love you, dark', a few times. I was never afraid of the dark again.

I tried the same thing with what I now think of as 'my lower self' – the parts of my character I didn't really like, or at least thought I didn't.

So I said, 'I love you David,' and after repeating it a few times, I realized that I not only loved David, I even liked David, my lower self.

This also helped me more fully understand that I really am not David as such – that is, not my lower self, which stands for a finite, material being.

I realize that I am my infinite higher self, pure Spirit or awareness. I am the knower of David, my lower self, and all other finite, ever-changing things. This has enabled me to 'Love David', and enjoy him a great deal!

This has also helped me immensely – to love everyone, and everything, constantly, which has and does brought such a 'peace' to all aspects of my life.

Applying love changed my life forever – and it can change yours as well.

Real Love

So…. What is love? I am referring to unconditional – in effect divine – love, not human, possessive love.

- Divine love is loving unconditionally – with loving kindness. TYG
- Real love – divine love – is selfless (egoless) and is free of fear. TYG
- Divine love pours itself upon the objects of its affections – just the way they are and without demanding anything in return. TYG

WHAT IS LOVE?

- Divine love is loving myself – just the way I am.
- Divine love is loving everyone – just the way they are.
- Divine love is the joy of giving, and giving unstintingly.
- Divine love is God in manifestation.
- Divine love is the acceptance of all beings, things and situations – just the way they are.
- Divine love is the source of all love – including human love.
- Divine love is all power.
- Love is the greatest power in the Cosmos, and with the practice of 'loving', one discovers that 'love power' is much more powerful than atomic power.

Human love, on the other hand, pales by comparison with it.

Another Example

I have woken up many mornings feeling great for the first minute or so, until the mind wakes up, and then the mental pressures create a 'not-feeling-good' feeling.

Well, the other day this happened at about 5:30 am, but the 'not-feeling-good' feeling was worse than I could ever recall. It was one of extreme negativity, so much so that it was actually frightening, and the negative thoughts were crowding in, one right after the other without stopping.

I fortunately soon recalled that I had to love all the thoughts just the way they are, and love the entire situation just the way it is. TYG

I loved every thought 'just the way it was', and I kept repeating these 'lovings'. I loved myself, over and over, as well, and I loved my global body repeatedly. I loved the pressure in my chest that the negativity had caused, just the way it is.

Soon 'bliss' appeared! It was with me within approximately five minutes, and I went back to a blissful sleep for about an hour. TYG

Upon my reawakening, the same thing happened, and I repeated all the same type of 'lovings' and the bliss came back, and I slept some more. TYG

I awoke, and arose at 7:30 am loving all, and loving the day before me just the way it is. TYG

I prayed that I would love all my trials throughout the day just the way they are. TYG

I did love every one of my trials, throughout that day just the way they were, including every thought, every feeling, and everything in the whole cosmos, just the way everything was and is.

I enjoyed a most wonderful day.

Summary

- God is love – love is Light.
- Divine love is all-giving.
- Divine love is unconditional.
- Divine love is loving everyone – equally.
- Divine love is the love we feel for all others, and for all things and situations just the way they are.
- Divine love can be measured by how much love we give to others.
- When you love your enemy, you find that you have no enemies.
- When we give love, we receive love – because what we give out must come back.

Loving Natural Things

I was with a friend on a recent occasion when she told me about a foal that had just been born at her farm, and how her daughter was extremely worried about its survival. My friend could not get back to her home for another two days, and said she was at her wits' end with worry about her daughter and the foal.

I took the opportunity to explain 'loving' just the way it is.

Well, she was hesitant about this idea, which was new to her; but as I asked her, what did she have to lose?, she admitted, nothing – except the foal, and maybe a nervous breakdown in her daughter, who was very emotional about the whole thing.

I told her about a couple of similar things to which I had applied 'loving just the way it is', and how everything had worked out. I also told her that now was the time to put her logical mind aside, and go with her heart. She agreed to try it. I then suggested the following loving words for her to apply,

'I love the struggles for life just the way they are – the struggles that my foal is experiencing now.' TYG

'I love the nervous stress that my emotional daughter is experiencing now, just the way it is.' TYG

I advised her to repeat these statements of love, and any other similar ones that came to her, several times from that moment throughout the evening.

I also told her that I would also make some 'lovings' for them that night as well.

She called me the next day, and she was delighted to be able to tell me, that the foal got over its crisis during the night, and her daughter was of course totally relieved, and at peace. TYG

She became a believer in 'loving everything just the way everything is' from then on! TYG

Some Thoughts

- The powerful effect of loving is instantly obvious. TYG
- When you know it, love is effortless. Hate is hard work. TYG
- Love is happiness. If we are not happy, we are not loving. TYG
- When you apply love to any problem or situation, the problem resolves. TYG
- Unconditional love is flowing with the universe, instead of resisting it. TYG
- Unconditional love is accepting yourself and

others – just the way you all are. TYG
- Unconditional love dissolves … all separateness. TYG
- Unconditional love dissolves … all resistance. TYG
- Love is the doorway to enlightenment. x3 TYG

Further Ideas to Meditate on

I have found that the more I practise loving myself just the way I am – and all others as well – the more my vibrations seem to rise to the higher dimensions. TYG (There's more about this in the next two chapters.)

I have also found that the more I love – the more my energy takes on the smoother finer vibrations of the higher dimensions – and I consciously realize that I am my higher self. x3 TYG

Affirmations

Again, to plant this technique deep in yourself, you may like to repeat to yourself aloud – over, and over, maybe one section at a time – the following.

With loving kindness:
1. I love the day before me – just the way it is. x3 IYG
2. My real love – divine love – is selfless (egoless) and I am free of fear. H&N x3 IYG
3. My love is all power – my love is all giving. H&N x3 IYG
4. God is love – love is light. x3 IYG
5. My divine love is unconditional. x3 IYG

With loving kindness:
6. Divine love is the love I feel for all others, and for all things and situations just the way they are. x3 IYG
7. I love everyone just the way they are. x3 IYG
8. I love my enemies just the way they are – and then I find that I have no enemies. x3 IYG
9. I love myself just the way I am. x3 IYG

10. The more I love myself, the more I am being my higher self. x3 IYG

With loving kindness:

11. When I give love, I receive love – because what I give out must come back. x3 IYG

12. When I apply love to any problem or situation – the problem resolves. x3 IYG

13. Love is effortless – hate is hard work. x3 IYG

14. Unconditional love is flowing with the universe – instead of resisting it. x3 IYG

With loving kindness:

15. Unconditional love is accepting myself and all others – just the way we all are. x3 IYG

16. My unconditional love dissolves … all separateness. x3 IYG

17. My unconditional love dissolves … all resistance. x3 IYG

18. The more I practise loving myself unconditionally just the way I am, and all others just the way *they* are, the more our vibrations rise to higher dimensions. x3 IYG

19 The more I love – the more I am free. x3 IYG

AFFIRMATION CHANT
I am loving kindness – in action in me now.
I am loving kindness – to God alone, I bow.
I am loving kindness – in mighty cosmic power.
I am the light of God – shining every hour.
I am loving kindness – shining like a sun:
I am God's sacred power – freeing everyone. x3 TYG

NOTES

CHAPTER THREE

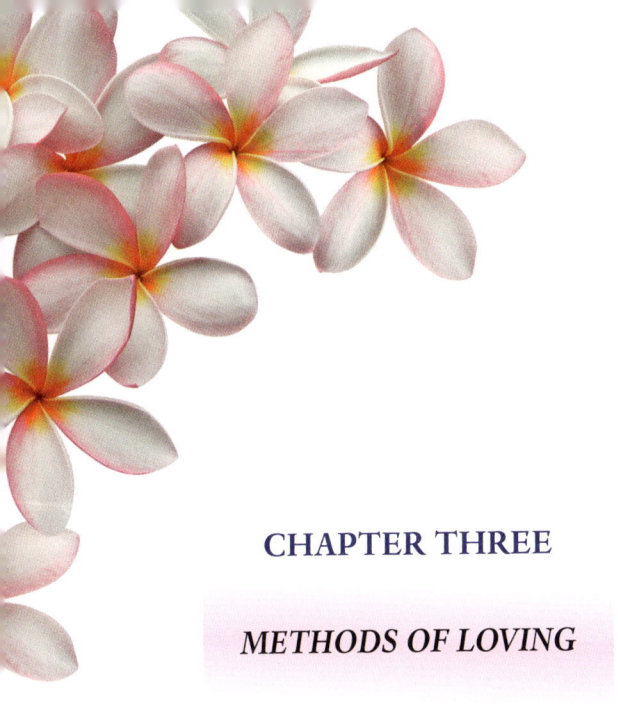

METHODS OF LOVING

An Experience of Loving

I'VE TRIED to explain how feeling surrounded by love as a child set me up in life, as I grew to be an adult. Except for the experience with the dark, I didn't have any sort of technique for working with love, though. It was just a sort of intuition I had, that love was everything that mattered. Something about that idea seemed to work, because I think that when I came to business I didn't approach it with fears about how things would be, I approached it with loving enjoyment. And somehow that must be what successful business is all about. Before I knew what was going on, I had made it work sufficiently to sell up and come back to Great Britain, so that my children would have the experience of growing up there.

I was always a spiritual seeker, I guess, and the story I now want to tell is important to me because it was one of the first times I really encountered love in action, in a way that was so uncomplicated as to be completely obvious to me. This turned out to be quite a major event in my life, and is connected to the spiritual teacher White Eagle. It took place in the south of England, where the White Eagle Lodge has its principal centre. I shall describe it in some detail, because I want to convey the whole atmosphere of love that I experienced.

After reading and enjoying White Eagle's wonderful book, THE LIVING WORD OF ST JOHN (of which more in the next chapter), I decided to visit the White Eagle Lodge in Hampshire. I called beforehand and asked, 'Is it possible to come to the Lodge, and have a talk with someone there?'. I was told that that day (a Tuesday) there would be a 'Healing Service' in the chapel, and I would be welcome. They held regular such services there three days a week.

I arrived at a very nice country house, and I was ushered into a living room in which a few other visitors had gathered. We were all enjoying a cup of tea and a very pleasant lady in a long blue gown was mingling with the visitors. She came up to me, touched my hand lightly and said quietly to herself, 'stressed'. She asked me if I would be taking healing, and I nervously replied 'No, I am just here to observe'. She then moved on to visit others, and when she had gone I said to myself, 'What is wrong with you, David? – If anyone needs healing, it's you'.

Shortly thereafter we were all invited into the healing chapel, and as I was going in I saw a young man in a white tunic, and I told him that I would like to have healing after all. He directed me to sit in a particular area where those wanting healing sat, and I sat down among them in an aisle seat.

At the front of the chapel, looking towards the people there for healing as well as those observing, was the lady in the blue gown. Directly in front of her were eight or so upholstered stools, where people who had come for healing would be invited to sit at the appropriate time. When the stools had been filled, healers in white tunics would one by one stand behind the patients. Each patient had been given a white card, filled in so as to describe the particular problem or problems that that person was suffering, and their healing prescription, described in the language of colour rays.

The person in the blue gown commenced the healing service with an opening prayer.

The healer for each patient read the person's 'card' so that they knew where to direct the healing angels' coloured rays. Then they applied the healing through their hands, touching or not quite touching the appropriate spot and projecting the colours with the imagination. The healing went on for ten or fifteen minutes and ended with some words of thanks to God each time. The whole service ended with a prayer by the person in the blue gown, and some gentle and wonderful music was played, which was conducive to meditation.

I learnt that patients would come again as often as they liked until they felt their healing was complete. There is no charge for the healing services or treatment whatsoever, but those who wish can make a contribution. I learnt that using the colours is like applying love in the form of light, except that the light has been broken up into the colours of the spectrum as though through a prism.

The entire service is one of great peace, and love, and whether you take healing or not, you most certainly feel very peaceful and well, just for being present at the service.

Almost immediately upon sitting down for the

service and without trying at all, I went into a very deep meditative state, wherein I thought that I was going to float off the seat, but I was so blissful that I wasn't bothered if I did. I did not, of course.

I also saw very clearly in my mind's eye, above my head but in front of me, a large oval opening about three feet high, in which I saw my father really clearly in full colour. He had passed on eight or ten months previously in the United States and had never been to the White Eagle Lodge in England, and to my knowledge had never known of its existence during his lifetime.

My Dad was beaming down at me, and I got the distinct feeling that he was very pleased indeed that I was at the White Eagle Lodge. He also wanted me to bring my Mother to healing services. I received these messages clearly, without a word being uttered, and I was very happy indeed.

After the service, I drove to my mother's house in Horsham and told her in detail of my experience, and about Dad's wishes. She was delighted, and I took her on Thursday for our first service together at the White Eagle Lodge in Hampshire, and I continued to take her to many, many services – all of which we both enjoyed very much.

All of the above experiences were totally steeped

in wonderful feelings of divine love, which I feel very strongly as I write these words.

Methods of Loving

I shall now go on to discuss 'methods of loving.'

There are many ways to love, but I shall only mention the ones that I use often, and which

- are very easy to practise, and
- are the most powerful ones that I know.

You can simply state your love of anyone, anything and everything, or any situation – *just the way it is or they are* – repetitively, and either silently, or by the spoken word. The spoken word is definitely the more powerful.

I do this constantly.

Examples:

I love you, Helen* – just the way you are. TYG

I love you, (name your self) – just the way you are. TYG

I love this physical body – just the way it is. TYG

I love this global body – just the way it is. TYG

I love this feeling – just the way it is. TYG

I love this fear – just the way it is. TYG

* The name of anyone you wish to think of.

Thoughts to Explore

I quite often refer to my 'global body' rather than to a 'part' of my body. For instance, if I had back pain, I might say, 'I love you, global body – just the way you are' – which gives me a picture of my entire body from top to toe, and I don't focus on the back pain in particular. TYG

'Just the way you are' lets the global body look after all of itself, including the back pain – which indeed it is perfectly capable of doing, as it was designed to do. TYG

Global Loving

I love London – just the way it is. TYG
I love Canada – just the way it is. TYG
I love the USA – just the way it is. TYG
I love you, Tony – just the way you are. TYG
I love you, Margaret – just the way you are. TYG
I love this government – just the way it is. TYG
I love you, David Cameron – just the way you are. TYG
I love you, Hitler – just the way you are. TYG

Every once in a while I deliberately say 'I love you Hitler – just the way you are' – or else someone else with that kind of a history. I do this to remind myself that God our Father loves Hitler or anyone else, no matter what they have done, and this includes myself – whatever *I've* done. It helps build my perspective, that loving really is 'loving – just the way it is', and I can love anyone, and everything, no matter what, just like God our Father does. TYG

I love you, England – just the way you are. TYG

I love work – just the way it is. TYG

I love the pain in my lower back – just the way it is. TYG

I also can love the pain in my lower back directly – just the way it is. TYG I try different approaches all the time, as I am sure you will! Here goes:

I love you, Stalin – just the way you are. TYG

I love my health – just the way it is. TYG

I love life – just the way it is. TYG

I love football – just the way it is. TYG

I love swine flu (or whatever the latest threatened epidemic is) – just the way it is. TYG

I love healthiness – just the way it is. TYG

I love illness – just the way it is. TYG

I love studying – just the way it is. TYG

The list of what you can love – just the way the things are – is endless. TYG

The benefits to everyone including yourself from loving everyone and everything – just the way they are – is so immense, it is beyond description. TYG

The Love Blanket

Another very successful method I use constantly to apply love or light to all people, things (or parts of things), and situations, is by imagining myself enfolding that person, thing, or situation in a transparent blanket of love or light. I find this enfolding technique very powerful indeed. I carefully enfold, or wrap the person or situation in a transparent blanket of love. I do it slowly and very lovingly. The more I practise this enfolding technique, the better I get at visualizing the person or situation, and the blanket of love wrapping around them. It brings me great peace and wellbeing. TYG

Here are some thoughts about practising the 'Blanket of Love' technique.
- Visualize enfolding any person, thing, or situation in a transparent blanket of love or light, and then 'leaving everything to God'. TYG
- You can help those whom you know are

suffering either physically or mentally, by enfolding the person with love or light. TYG
- Enfold that soul tenderly with love or light, and talk to him or her on the inner spiritual level – that is, in your heart. TYG
- Give the person courage through love – which is the spirit of Christ. TYG

Another Way of Applying Love

I often talk silently to the person I am enfolding with the blanket of love. I tell them that I love them, just the way they are, just as God our Father loves him or her – unconditionally, just the way they are. I tell them to be courageous, that all will be well. I tell him or her to 'Let go, and let God'.

On one occasion, I was enfolding a soul who was not feeling very well at all with the blanket of love. I loved her for a few minutes in this way, and within half an hour, she was altogether better, and feeling very good. If it is a much more serious illness or situation, the loving might take more time. Nevertheless, when I persist, I have never seen it fail to bring forth God's miracles. TYG

METHODS OF LOVING

- Loving kindness is strong. TYG
- Loving kindness is accurate. TYG
- Loving kindness is intelligent. TYG
- Loving kindness is lenient. TYG
- Loving kindness is unconditional. TYG
- Loving kindness, loves. TYG
- Loving kindness is the divine solution of every pain, and every problem. TYG

When you are loving, you are letting go, and you are letting loving kindness resolve it. TYG

Try loving kindness, apply loving kindness – and you will love loving kindness.

When you are 'loving', as in the techniques I have just described, you are allowing the vibration of whatever you are loving to be raised – but, at the same time, you are raising your own vibration as well, by opening your heart and loving whatever it might be. TYG

When you are practising loving, you will feel good, and you will experience more aliveness, more expansion, more renewal. TYG

You will open your heart more, and more, by loving yourself with loving kindness. TYG

You will relax more, so that you feel less tired.

Affirmations

Repeat to yourself aloud – over, and over:

With loving kindness:

1. I love you (your own name) – just the way you are. x3 IYG
2. I love this physical body – just the way it is. x3 IYG
3. I love this global body – just the way it is. x3 IYG
4. I love this etheric body – just the way it is. x3 IYG

With loving kindness:

5. I love this mental body – just the way it is. x3 IYG
6. I love this emotional body – just the way it is. x3 IYG
7. I love these feelings – just the way they are. x3 IYG

With loving kindness:

8. I love all my thoughts – both the positive ones and the negative ones – just the way they are. x3 IYG

9. I love all my limited, and fearful thoughts – just the way they are. x3 TYG

10. I love my etheric body – just the way it is. x3 TYG

11. I love all my urgencies – just the way they are. x3 TYG

12. I love all my desires – just the way they are. x3 TYG

13. I love all my ego – just the way it is. x3 TYG

14. I meditate on love. x3 TYG

15. I absorb love. x3 TYG

With loving kindness:

16. I give love – and my soul becomes alight. x3 TYG

17. I know that love is not possessive. x3 TYG

18. I know that to love is to give. x3 TYG

19. I see love as a radiation – a sending forth from the heart – a sweet essence which heals. x3 TYG

20. I give love to all – just the way they are. x3 TYG

21. I radiate love to all – just the way they are. x3 TYG

22. I love everything – just the way everything is. x3 TYG

23. I love every situation – just the way every

situation is. x3 TYG

24. I love this depressive feeling – just the way it is. x3 TYG

25. I love this loving feeling – just the way its is.

AFFIRMATION CHANT
I am loving kindness – in action in me now.
I am loving kindness – to God alone, I bow.
I am loving kindness – in mighty cosmic power.
I am the light of God – shining every hour.
I am loving kindness – shining like a sun:
I am God's sacred power – freeing everyone. x3 TYG

NOTES/LOVE LIST

NOTES

CHAPTER FOUR

LOVE YOUR SELF

THIS IS a story about remembering things which are helpful and nourishing for you. In Chapter 3, I mentioned going to White Eagle Lodge on the strength of a book. A friend had given me a copy and it had a huge positive influence on me. It was THE LIVING WORD OF ST JOHN by White Eagle, and it contains detailed interpretations of St John's Gospel. White Eagle is a very practical spiritual teacher who spoke through Grace Cooke for over fifty years and the teaching in this book started to come through in the middle of the blitz on London in World War II. This book shows the wonderful spiritual harmony that exists between the modern teacher White Eagle and St John, the writer of the Gospel.

The Gospel of St John itself is different from the other three Gospels, in that within it Jesus describes the purpose of his work on earth. It is an amazing work, and it certainly impacted my life. If you haven't read it, I certainly recommend you do.

Jesus taught and demonstrated a great deal about love, which White Eagle interprets from the Bible in very understandable terms. He made it possible that we can all understand what divine love means – and relate to and apply these great teachings of divine love by Jesus the Christ.

I moved to Britain a second time in 1973 – this time to live – and I was going through a depressing time of nervous tension and turmoil, which related to business matters. I was really 'down', and suddenly I remembered that I had packed away this book and brought it to England with me. I was drawn to the book like a magnet to steel, and felt strongly that I needed to read it. I unearthed it among my packing cases.

For two or three years I was never far away from THE LIVING WORD OF ST JOHN and I read pieces from it at every opportunity, every day. I carried it with me everywhere. I learned a great deal about applying love from it, and from reading it I began to practise applying love more regularly and deliberately, with great success.

I practise this loving now in almost all similar situations with everyone, and I enjoy life much, much more as a result.

I wrote LOVING EVERY MOMENT because discovering these 'loving' truths and seeing how they changed my life made me want to share them.

1 John 3:11
For this is the message that ye heard from the beginning, that we should love one another. TYG

Going up the Ladder

One thing that the book on St John's Gospel taught me is that we can function on many different levels of life. There is the everyday world where our minds are dominant, but there are also worlds of awareness that do not require physical forms, only consciousness breathed into life, though they are just as real as the physical world. They just vibrate to a different frequency – a higher frequency. I found that through my loving I could mount a ladder and live a bit more among those higher frequencies – to the place where my 'higher self' lives.

A Practice using Frequency

We have touched on 'loving yourself' in the previous chapter, but here we shall take it much further.

You are your 'higher self' – pure spirit, awareness, light, but still essentially you. Once you accept this truth, then there is really nothing else for you to identify with.

You become aware that all other identities (for instance, the lower self, made up of the etheric, physical, mental, and emotional bodies/layers) are transient, mortal things – they are forever changing and always dissolve.

It is only the light within you, the centre that is God, that is eternal and unchanging.

When you love yourself, you are being your higher self. You are rising in what I call 'frequency', like waves. The more I practise 'loving' myself, the more I rise in 'frequency' to my higher self. It is like I am going up a ladder or scale. I love to say aloud many times each day and night from my the vantage point of my higher self, 'I love you, David, just the way you are'. TYG I am consciously being my reality. I am consciously being myself my higher self, the Christ Light. *I am That I am*, as Jesus said. TYG

I believe it is very important to love your self

(your real self, and through it your everyday self) – just the way it is. TYG

An Exercise to Do Now

Love all of yourself – just the way you are:
- Love (your name) – just the way you are. TYG
- Love (your etheric body) – just the way it is. TYG
- Love (your physical body) – just the way it is. TYG
- Love (your emotional body) – just the way it is. TYG
- Love (your mental body) – just the way it is. TYG
- Love (your thoughts) – just the way they are. TYG
- Love (your global body) – just the way it is. TYG
- Love all your trials – just the way they are. TYG
- Love all your experiences – just the way they are. TYG

1 Corinthians 13:7
Love never gives up, never loses faith, is always hopeful, and endures through every circumstance.

Another Story

One morning I was feeling very poorly, so I loved myself just the way I am. TYG Then I loved the sick feeling, just the way it is. TYG

Then I loved the 'poor me' feeling, just the way it is. TYG

I repeated these affirmations of love several times throughout the morning, and I then felt better. I gave my feelings a hand up the ladder, from the start.

These days, I don't hang on to my negative feelings. I love them right away just the way they are, for as long as it takes to move them up the scale in frequency. But, be assured – they will move up.

So, to spell it out: love all your positive aspects, and love all your negative ones as well!

Repeat to yourself over, and over:
I love you (your name) – just the way you are. TYG
I love you (your name) – just the way you are. TYG
I love you (your name) – just the way you are. TYG
I love you (your name) – just the way you are. TYG

I love you (your name) – just the way you are. TYG
I love you (your name) – just the way you are. TYG

If any thought then arises, state: I love this thought – just the way it is. TYG

More you Can Work on

There are more things you can bring 'up the frequency ladder'.

I find it great to love my thoughts, particularly if a negative or judgmental thought arises. I just say, 'I love you, thought – just the way you are', and it's gone. I don't berate myself for having it. If it's a deeply ingrained, troublesome thought, I love it more, by stating my love for it a few more times, or several more times. I treat doubts the same way. Any doubt that arises, I state:

I love this doubt – just the way it is. TYG

Any fear that arises, I state:

I love this fear – just the way it is. TYG

I find it very important to love my fears, too. Fear is the biggest generator of negative feelings, and situations, as well as all diseases. The more I practise 'loving' my fears, the faster I have become at coaxing them 'up the frequency ladder', so to speak. I don't nurture my fears, I love them right away – just the way they are – for as long as it takes to move them up the ladder. TYG Any confusion that arises, I state:

I love this confusion – just the way it is. TYG

Any depression that arises, I state:

I love this depression – just the way it is. TYG

And, maybe most importantly, I find it very helpful to love my depressions. Depression is one of the biggest generators of negative feelings, and situations, and it too is a generator of diseases. The more I practise 'loving' my depressions, the faster I have been able to help them rise to a higher frequency. I don't hold on to my depressions, I love them right away just the way they are, and for as long as it takes to 'move them up'. TYG

If any feelings arise, whatever they may be, I state:

I love this feeling – just the way it is. TYG

Any anger that arises, I state:

I love this anger – just the way it is. TYG

I find that anger, too, is very important to avoid – as much as I possibly can. Anger is another major generator of negative energies, feelings, and situations, and therefore of diseases. The more I practise 'loving my anger', the more I help it to rise up into higher frequencies. I certainly try to avoid anger – but I love it right away whenever it appears, just the way it is. I am finding that the more I love, the less anger appears. TYG

Any egotism that arises, I state:

I love this egotism – just the way it is. TYG

I could go on, and on about ego. I find that it is really important to keep control of my ego, and I do so – by loving it.

I love you, ego – just the way you are. TYG

A Story about Ego

One day I was having a conversation with a dear friend, and I found myself getting a bit hot under the collar about her criticizing my point of view. My ego felt bruised. So I left the room for a moment, and loved my ego, by stating, 'I love you, ego – just the way you are', a few times. I also forgave her for her criticisms, and I sent her love, by stating a few times, 'I love you – just the way you are'. I also forgave myself for my egotistical attitude, and I poured love on the situation by stating a few times, 'I love you, David's ego – just the way you are'. This whole application took less than five minutes, and I quickly felt much better. TYG

I then returned, and all was well. Her attitude seemed to have changed. Mine certainly had, as I realized that her comments were not criticisms, but were actually constructive comments – for which I thanked her. The rest of the discussion was a great pleasure. TYG

Love your Humanity, as well as your Divinity

Besides being divine, we are also human, including all the bits and pieces that make up humanness, such as all our personal imperfections that arise on occasion, such as egotism. But I love all my imperfections as they arise, and I am grateful to them for giving me the reason to state my love for them, and rise in frequency with them.

- I love you, David's imperfections – just the way you are. TYG
- I love my humanness at every opportunity. That is why we are here – to learn to do that.

Of course, we all love our divinity, easily! – but I still state,

- I love you, David's divinity – just the way you are. TYG
- And so, love your insecurities and your negative and positive feelings – just the way they are. TYG

Our Forgiving Nature

If you feel unforgiving of anyone, including yourself, forgive the unforgivingness – just the way it is. TYG

If you feel un-loving of anyone or hatred for them – including yourself – forgive these feelings, even the way they are. TYG

With loving kindness, love all your imperfections. Here's how it works.

- You can change them by loving them. TYG
- You can't change them by denying or hating or fearing them.

- Denying or hating or fearing is resistance.
- Resistance only builds up whatever was the cause of the suffering.
- Loving them or anything – just the way they are – allows them and assists them to change into positive expressions.

Our Thoughts are Where all Things Begin

With loving kindness, love all your thoughts – both the positive ones and the negative ones.

Love all your limited, and fearful thoughts. Love your weaknesses as well as your strengths, for weaknesses are the areas of your being that most need your love to evolve.

It is very important to love all your thoughts, the positive and negative ones alike. The negative thoughts can be a major generator of negative energies, feelings, and situations, as well as diseases. if not kept under control. The more I practise 'loving' my thoughts, the more I help them to rise up into higher frequencies and thereby I bypass the negative energies, feelings, and situations, as well as the diseases that they help generate. I certainly try to avoid negativity – but I love it right away whenever it appears as a thought or feeling. I am finding that the more I love, the less negativity appears.

With loving kindness, concentrate most of all on loving yourself:

Repeat to yourself, over, and over:

With loving kindness:
- I love you (your name) – just the way you are (I am) TYG
- I cannot love too much. TYG

Think of your positive and negative thoughts, and fears, and your angers, and egotistic intrusions as little children that need love and reassurance in order that their vibrations be raised out of limitation into the higher frequencies. TYG

★

I find that it is really important to love myself just the way I am. When I first tried to love myself, I found it difficult, and thought I was being quite self-centred. I wanted to love the person I wanted to be. I was having a very difficult time at that moment.

Eventually, I loved myself just the way I am, and then I tried loving myself just the way I am several more times. I repeated these 'lovings' over and over a few times, and I started to feel better. TYG

After a few more, I became really relaxed and felt wonderful. All the resistance had been dissolved. I use this continuously whenever I need it, which is still most days. I never have had any doubt about loving myself since the first time.

I also have come to realize that God my Father loves me just the way I am, so that's what I can do, too – love myself just the way I am. TYG

Affirmations

The range of things you can bring love to is huge. Use whichever of the following relate to where you are, or make up your own, and repeat the affirmations yourself aloud, over and over:

With loving kindness:
1. I love that everything is predetermined – just the way it is. x3 TYG
2. Within a tube of light I enfold my lower self – just the way it is. x3 TYG
3. I love my higher self and my universe – just the way I am. x3 TYG
4. I love my lower self and its world – just the

way they are. x3 IYG

5. I love you (your own name) – just the way you are. x3 IYG

6. I love all of myself – just the way I am. x3 IYG

With loving kindness:

7. By loving every person – just the way they are – I find peace with every person. x3 IYG

8. By loving my negative feelings, just the way they are, I find peace with myself. x3 IYG

9. By loving my nervousness – just the way it is – I find peace with myself. x3 IYG

10. With light I enfold ……….. – just the way ………….. is. x3 IYG

11. I love you, (someone else's name) – just the way you are. x3 IYG

12. I love you, anger – just the way *you* are. x3 IYG

With loving kindness:

13. I love you, impatience – just the way you are. x3 IYG

14. I love you, fear – just the way you are. x3 IYG

15. I love you, global body – just the way you

are. ✿x3 IYG

16. I love you, etheric body – just the way you are. ✿x3 IYG

17. I love you, physical body – just the way you are. ✿x3 IYG

18. I love you, mental body – just the way you are. ✿x3 IYG

19. I love you, emotional body – just the way you are. ✿x3 IYG

20. I love all thoughts – just the way they are. ✿x3 IYG

21. I love my feelings – just the way they are. ✿x3 IYG

22. I love all sad and happy feelings, and any other feelings – just the way they are. ✿x3 IYG

23. I love all my trials – just the way they are. ✿x3 IYG

24. I love all my experiences – just the way they are. ✿x3 IYG

With loving kindness:

25. I simply love every single thing – just the way it is. ✿x3 IYG

26. I love all beings – just the way they are. ✿x3 IYG

27. I love all my judgments – just the way they

are. x3 IYG

28. I love all my joys and discomforts – just the way they are. x3 IYG

29. I love everything that happens – just the way it happens. x3 IYG

30. I love all things – just the way they are. x3 IYG

31. I love my humanity – just the way it is. x3 IYG

32. I love my divinity – just the way it is. x3 IYG

With loving kindness:

33. I love all God's plan for me – just the way it is. x3 IYG

34. I love all my successes and disappointments – just the way they are. x3 IYG

35. I love all life – just the way it is. x3 IYG

36. I love all gas blockages – just the way they are. x3 IYG

37. I love all souls – just the way they are. x3 IYG

38. I love this soul – just the way it is. x3 IYG

39. I love all pluses and minuses – just the way they are. x3 IYG

40. I love all my central nervous system – just the way it is. x3 IYG

With loving kindness:

41. I love each and every agitation – just the way it is. x3 IYG

42. I love everyone and everything – just the way they are. x3 IYG

43. I see and experience love's inner peace reflected everywhere. x3 IYG

44. I am love–light – just the way I am. x3 IYG

45. I am peace – just the way I am. x3 IYG

46. I am happiness – just the way I am. x3 IYG

47. I am all forgiven – just the way I am. x3 IYG

With loving kindness:

48. I forgive all – just the way all are. x3 IYG

49. I love my fear of being alone – just the way it is. x3 IYG

50. I live love–light – just the way I am. x3 IYG

51. I love my pure awareness (emptiness) – just the way I am. x3 IYG

52. I continuously love every person – every thing – every situation – just the way each one is. x3 IYG

With loving kindness:

53. I love you (your name) – just the way you are. x3 IYG

54. I love you (your name) – just the way you are. x3 IYG
55. I love you (your name) – just the way you are. x3 IYG
56. I love you (your name) – just the way you are. x3 IYG
57. I love you (your name) – just the way you are. x3 IYG
58. I love you (your name) – just the way you are. x3 IYG

AFFIRMATION CHANT
I am loving kindness – in action in me now.
I am loving kindness – to God alone, I bow.
I am loving kindness – in mighty cosmic power.
I am the light of God – shining every hour.
I am loving kindness – shining like a sun:
I am God's sacred power – freeing everyone. x3 IYG

NOTES

CHAPTER FIVE

LOVING RELATIONSHIPS

AFTER I met my wife, Uranda, in 1983/84, we began to discuss spiritual matters – and it was this that led me to the thought that I could or should write down what I had been fortunate enough to learn over the years. Uranda subsequently encouraged me with this thought.

Uranda and I led a very spiritual life together. We were not religious, in that we rarely went to church, but 'spiritual' is a good word to describe us, in that we often had wonderful discussions together about our spiritual views and practices. We read aloud to each other from spiritual books that attracted us.

My life with Uranda and all that we had been

through and learned together has added immeasurably to the practice of 'loving,' by requiring me actually to practise the power of loving. Close relationships always demand hard work!

For instance, I used my technique of 'loving' on several occasions when Uranda and I were having disagreements, which sometimes became emotional. I learned, on these occasions, to practise 'loving Uranda', and almost immediately the disagreement disappeared.

I also learned to 'love the situation', whatever it was, and it immediately became resolved to the benefit of all concerned.

I also learned to 'love David', and almost immediately the disagreement disappeared.

1 Corinthians 13:13
Three things will last forever – faith – hope – and love – and the greatest of these is love.

Emotions

Emotions play a very big part in our everyday life. As well as being able to bring us much joy and happiness, they can on occasion cause us a great deal of discomfort and unhappiness.

When emotions are added to ego-generated desires, the final shape is unalterably cast. So it is very important carefully to select our ideas – which are our thought-forms – to see if we really want them, before we add emotion to the mix.

Of course, everything depends on whether we select positive emotions or negative ones – which will be according to what we really want.

Far from being a problem, emotions are a great blessing in this earthly life, when we learn to control them – by being aware of their arising at the moment it is happening, and releasing them immediately by loving them if they aren't the ones we want. Do not entertain the negativity.

We can regain complete control of our emotions, just by 'loving them'.

Here is a helpful thought from the twentieth-century teacher Ramana Maharshi, one that helps me a great deal.

'Everything is predetermined.

'But one is always free not to identify oneself with the body.

'And one is also always free not to be affected by

the pleasure and pain associated with the body's activities.'

Some More Thoughts

Emotions are most certainly associated with the activities of the body. Here's how it works.

When we consciously realize
- that the 'body' is a transient device, a kind of 'terminal' in the computer sense;
- that we are much more than just our 'terminal' type of body';
- that we are Spirit (pure awareness or consciousness) – free of the body/ego,

then we are able to choose not to be affected by the pleasure and pain associated with the terminal body's activities.

*

One of the leading items to come under the heading 'pain' is emotion. It is very important to love all our emotions with loving kindness – just the way they are. TYG

When you love your emotions, you are *being* your higher self. TYG

The more I practise 'loving' my emotions with loving kindness – the more I consciously rise in frequency to realize that *I am my higher self.* TYG

I love to say aloud, many times each day and night from my higher self:

'With loving kindness I love you, emotional body – just the way you are.' TYG

When I love my emotional body with loving kindness – just the way it is – I am consciously keeping my emotional body quiet, and under control. I am also being my reality – I am consciously being my higher self, the Christ Light. *I AM That I AM*, said Jesus.

Just as it is extremely important to love everyone and everything – just the way they are – it is also very, very important to love all emotions – just the way *they* are. TYG

Now here are a few of the most disruptive emotions – ones that regularly cause us all problems, whether in the having or the not having them:

fear
shame
impatience
greed
guilt
desire

nervousness
pride
anger
rage
joy
anticipation
love
hate
patience
humility
sympathy
happiness
suffering
apathy
empathy.

When any one of these is attached to an ego's desire – then all hell can break loose, and most certainly does!

An ego is always attached to a body.

*

It is almost impossible to remove these emotions from our lives altogether, but you most certainly can 'love them with loving kindness' – just the way they are' when they do appear.

Utilizing the 'loving kindness' way, you will remain calm, cool, and harmonized, and will avoid being affected by the pain – associated with the emotional ego's activities. TYG

Loving Fears

Recently, I was feeling very nervous about what a particular person might be doing to my house, and I became quite fearful. The more I entertained this fear, the more nervous I became, so:

With loving kindness:
- I loved my nervousness just the way it is. TYG
- Then I loved the fear, just the way it is. TYG
- Then I loved the nervous ego, just the way it is. TYG
- Then I loved the fear ego, just the way it is. TYG

I repeated these affirmations of love several times and I then began to feel better. I repeated them several more times – and then they disappeared and I felt I was whole. TYG

I don't hang on to my emotions, and I love them right away just the way they are TYG , for as long as it takes to move them up in frequency. TYG

Love All your Negative and Positive Emotions

As souls temporarily embodied in physical vehicles, we bring with us the blueprint of our past issues from previous life-experiences. And emotions are one part of this blueprint. That is why certain things, situations, a person, and so on, can stir our emotions – and we don't know why. Or, we can become addicted in some way – even though we know deep down that it is not healthy to do so.

I now look at these types of situations as indicators to help me to resolve issues I have in this lifetime. We have the power to release all the lower emotional frequencies by loving them – which frees them and transmutes them into love–light. TYG

Affirmations

Here's another long list of ideas as to what you can repeat to yourself, aloud, over and over, to maintain your practice:

With loving kindness:

1. I love my positive emotions – just the way they are. x3 TYG

LOVING RELATIONSHIPS

2. I love my negative emotions – just the way they are. x3 IYG

3. I love (your own name) – just the way I am. x3 IYG

4. I love all other emotional egos everywhere – just the way they are. x3 IYG

5. I love this emotional ego – just the way it is. x3 IYG

6. I love suppressed feelings – just the way they are. x3 IYG

7. I love sadness – just the way it is. x3 IYG

8. I love happiness – just the way it is. x3 IYG

9. I love joy with loving kindness – just the way it is. x3 IYG

10. I love all egos that are trapped in addiction – just the way they are. x3 IYG

11. I love my ego – just the way it is. x3 IYG

12. I love being free – just the way I am. x3 IYG

13. I love not being affected by the body's pleasures or pains – I love them just the way they are. x3 IYG

14. I love controlling my emotions by loving them just the way they are. x3 IYG

15. I love the pain generated by emotion – just the way it is. x3 IYG

16. I love all emotions – just the way they are.

x3 IYG

17. I love my emotions and I am being my higher self – just the way I am. x3 IYG

18. The more I practise 'loving' my emotions' – the more I consciously rise in frequency to realize that *I am my higher self.* x3 IYG

19. I love consciously being my higher self, the Christ Light. x3 IYG

20. It is important to me to love everyone and everything – just the way they are. x3 IYG

21. It is very, very important to me to love all emotions – just the way they are. x3 IYG

22. I love fear – just the way it is. x3 IYG

23. I love pain – just the way it is. x3 IYG

24. I love shame – just the way it is. x3 IYG

25. I love impatience – just the way it is. x3 IYG

26. I love greed – just the way it is. x3 IYG

27. I love guilt – just the way it is. x3 IYG

28. I love desire – just the way it is. x3 IYG

29. I love nervousness – just the way it is. x3 IYG

30. I love pride – just the way it is. x3 IYG

31. I love desire – just the way it is. x3 IYG

32. I love anger – just the way it is. x3 IYG

33. I love rage – just the way it is. x3 IYG

34. I love joy – just the way it is. x3 IYG

35. I love anticipation – just the way it is. x3 TYG
36. I love love – just the way it is. x3 TYG
37. I love hate – just the way it is. x3 TYG
38. I love patience – just the way it is. x3 TYG
39. I love humility – just the way it is. x3 TYG
40. I love sympathy – just the way it is. x3 TYG
41. I love happiness again – just the way it is. x3 TYG
42. I love suffering – just the way it is. x3 TYG
43. I love apathy – just the way it is. x3 TYG
44. I love empathy – just the way it is. x3 TYG

AFFIRMATION CHANT

I am loving kindness – in action in me now.
I am loving kindness – to God alone, I bow.
I am loving kindness – in mighty cosmic power.
I am the light of God – shining every hour.
I am loving kindness – shining like a sun:
I am God's sacred power – freeing everyone. x3 TYG

NOTES

CHAPTER SIX

UTILIZING THE DAILY LOVE LIST

I HAVE BEEN practising 'loving' and enjoying the benefits of doing so for quite some time now, and I found it so very successful in creating a much higher quality of life, that I have kept adding things to love.

This is alright in itself, but I started to have so many people, things, situations, etc., to love, that I could not remember them all when I wanted to send them 'love energy', so I devised a 'love list' that helps me immensely.

A 'love list' is exactly what the name implies, it's a list of people, things and situations that I like to send love to every day. I speak my love list every morning before I start my day. Soon after I began it, it was three pages long and it took between three and five minutes to say it.

I say my love list out loud, as my experience tells me that 'the spoken word' is much more powerful than the silent word. Speaking takes more energy than thinking, so when you 'speak it' you are putting more energy into your loving.

On page 110, I have attached a sample love list to help you formulate your own, should you wish to try it. I am sure you will find many wonderful benefits of applying love to whomsoever and whatever you care to.

This love list sample has many blank spaces which you need to fill in the words, names, etc., of those you wish to apply 'loving' to each day.

★

This chapter explains the importance of applying the practice of loving everyone, and all life and all your loved ones and situations on Planet Earth, and in the entire cosmic ocean repeatedly every day.

Now I am sure that you have heard this before:

Acts 20:35, words ascribed to Jesus
It is more blessed to give than to receive.

I believe that this statement is absolutely true. TYG

However, what we must realize is that when you truly 'give', you always receive back what you have given, multiplied many times. TYG

Of course Jesus loves every one of us with loving kindness – unconditionally – that is, just the way we are. TYG

And Jesus provides us with great examples of his totally, unconditionally loving everyone with loving kindness– just the way they are, by his demonstrating that he even loved those who were torturing and crucifying him. TYG

What a phenomenal example! It is a tough one to live up to – but we can do it, because we can love, just as Jesus has taught us. TYG

I feel that we are all subject to our own forms of crucifixion, that come up in our lives almost every day – but we can deal with them, as Jesus, did, and as Maitreya did, as Buddha did – by loving them all with loving kindness – just the way they are. TYG

★

Jesus truly is the 'ever-loving one'. He showed us the way to love everybody and every thing with loving kindness – and when we do, we are 'ever-loving ones' too.

We have another great example from Jesus, one that shows us he has received back, and continues to do so, the love that he gave on the cross, many millions, and billions of times, from all his devotees who have, and do follow his teachings. We all love him – millions of people from around the world – consciously love him every day 🌼 and of course his loving kindness comes back to us *all* every day.

Now all the applications of loving that have been presented here in the first few chapters are very applicable, and very good indeed, but we can also have one or two scheduled 'loving sessions' each day wherein you repetitively send love or light to anyone, everyone and anything that you might wish to, on an organized repetitive basis, not just when there is a problem. 🌼

I do my 'daily love' sessions as follows:
- The first one, every morning, as soon as I wake up, or shortly after. 🌼
- A second one, when I feel I want to, in bed as I am about to go to sleep. 🌼

It's best for the 'daily love' practice that you make a list which you can refer to each time you send love. 🌼 The positive loving results that are generated from both the love you send out to the recipients –

and the love that comes back to you from them – is immense. TYG What you send is multiplied several times by God. TYG

Without a list, it is pretty much impossible that any of us could remember all those persons and situations that you wish consciously to send love or light to each day. I did not use a list for years, but I found that my 'loving' of my loved ones, and other important matters and things was erratic. I could not remember everything every day – every day it changed, and many times people were left out, that I did not want to be left out. So the 'daily love list' was born, and it works well. TYG

The list helps you to be sure that you don't forget anyone (but if you do, love your forgetfulness!). TYG

Most days, I manage to send my list twice, and each time I do it, it puts me in a really great, blissful state. I really love it! TYG

Nowadays, my list is almost four pages, typed, but it still only takes ten to fifteen minutes to send it forth, and I find that it is really worth doing. TYG I feel so happy, doing my continuous love list, that I truly understand the phrase, 'love is giving'. It certainly is, but it all comes back not once but many times over. TYG

A Sample 'Daily Love List'

Here is an example that you can modify any way you like. It will help you get started. There are plenty of blanks for you to put the names of people or things in.

If you go to the website www.lovingeverymoment.com, you can download this 'Daily Love List' file as a Word file, which will allow you to modify it any way that suits you. Note also the blank pages at the end of this book.

Father–Mother – in blazing light:

I love: all ………'s tests this day – just the way they are. TYG

I love: all ………'s fears and fear of being alone this day – just the way they are. TYG

I love: ………'s etheric body this day – just the way it is. TYG

I love: ………'s mental body this day – just the way it is. TYG

I love: ………'s emotional body this day – just the way it is. TYG

I love: ………'s physical body this day – just the way it is. TYG

Father–Mother – in blazing light:

I love: ………'s nervous stomach this day – just the way it is. TYG

I love: all ………'s gas blockages and digestion system this day – just the way it is. TYG

I love: all ………'s money needs and money supplies this day – just the way it is. TYG

I love: all ………'s lower self and its world this day – just the way they are. TYG

Father–Mother – in blazing light:

I love: Planet Earth and all beings and all life upon it this day – just the way they are. TYG

I love: my dear Mum and Dad this day – just the way they are. TYG

I love: dear ……… and family this day – just the way they are. TYG

I love: ……., ………, ………, ………, ………, the dogs and cats this day. TYG

I love: ………, and ………, and all their families this day – just the way they are. TYG

Father–Mother – in blazing light:

I love: ………, and ………, this day – just the way they are. TYG

I love: ...., ..., ..., ..., ..., – just the way they are. TYG

I love: ...., and her family and pets this day – just the way they are. TYG

I love: ...., and his family and pets this day – just the way they are. TYG

I love: ...., ..., ..., ..., ..., ..., all the dogs, cats, horses, and other animals this day – just the way they are. TYG

I love: ...., and his/her partner this day – just the way they are. TYG

I love: every part of ....'s wonderful day and night, right now – just the way they are.

Father–Mother – in blazing light:

I love: the entire Cosmos and everyone and everything and within it this day – just the way they are. TYG

I love: ...., and family this day – just the way they are. TYG

I love: all the .... s (family name, or a social group) this day – just the way they are. TYG

I love: all the .... s this day – just the way they are. TYG

I love: all the .... s this day – just the way they are. TYG

UTILIZING THE 'DAILY LOVE LIST'

I love: all the ………s this day – just the way they are. TYG

I love: ………, and ……… this day – just the way they are. TYG

I love: ………, and family this day – just the way they are. TYG

Father–Mother – in blazing light:

I love: all the ………s this day – just the way they are. TYG

I love: all the ………s this day – just the way they are. TYG

I love: all the ………s this day – just the way they are. TYG

I love: ………, and family this day – just the way they are. TYG

I love: ………, and family this day – just the way they are. TYG

I love: my Transition, when it comes, and this day – just the way it is. TYG

Father–Mother – in blazing light:

I love: ………, and family this day – just the way they are. TYG

I love: ………, and family this day – just the way they are. TYG

I love: ………, and family this day – just the way they are. TYG

I love: ………, and family this day – just the way they are. TYG

I love: ………, and family this day – just the way they are. TYG

I love: ………, and family this day – just the way they are. TYG

Father–Mother – in blazing light:

I love: all ………'s colleagues and families this day – just the way they are. TYG

I love: all………'s personal affairs, this day – just the way they are. TYG

I love: all ………'s business affairs, this day – just the way they are. TYG

I love: ………, and family, this day – just the way they are. TYG

I love: ………, and family, this day – just the way they are. TYG

I love: ………, and family, this day – just the way they are. TYG

Father–Mother – in blazing light:

I love: all life, and life-forms in all the Cosmos this day – just the way they are. TYG

I love: all archangels, all angels, and all beings of light this day. TYG

I love: all ascended and unascended Masters this day. TYG

I love: world peace, this day – just the way it is. TYG

I love: President Obama, and his family and his government, and his 'govern by love' policy, this day – just the way they are. TYG

I love: all the politicians, whoever they are, and just the way they are. TYG

I love: every part of ……….'s wonderful body, this day – just the way they are. TYG

I love: every part of ……….'s wonderful body, this day – just the way they are. TYG

Father–Mother – in blazing light:

I love: baby, and friends this day – just the way they are. TYG

I love: the healing, taking place now in ……….'s ………., this day – just the way it is. TYG

I love: all ……….'s loving all – this day – just the way they are. TYG

I love: ………., and all ………., members this day – just the way they are. TYG

I love: Mr and Mrs ………., and family this day – just the way they are. TYG

I love: ...., and Mr ...., this day – just the way they are. TYG

I love: ...., and her two sons this day – just the way they are. TYG

I love: ...., and family, this day – just the way they are. TYG

This list is for your guidance and inspiration only. Modify it as much as you like, and if you wish use the blank pages at the end of the book to start a new list.

1 Corinthians 13:5
Love is not jealous, or boastful, or proud, or rude. It does not demand its own way. It is not irritable, and it keeps no record of being wronged. TYG

AFFIRMATION CHANT
I am loving kindness – in action in me now.
I am loving kindness – to God alone, I bow.
I am loving kindness – in mighty cosmic power.
I am the light of God – shining every hour.
I am loving kindness – shining like a sun:
I am God's sacred power – freeing everyone. x3 TYG

NOTES/LOVE LIST

NOTES/LOVE LIST

CHAPTER SEVEN

LOVING EVERY MOMENT

EVERYONE is searching for happiness almost continuously, and we do find it in many ways, at different times, and for varying periods.

However – to most people – happiness seems to be spasmodic. But, by loving, happiness is continuously available to us all – every moment of every day.

Our Creator has given all of us a most wonderful gift. He has given us the opportunity to love all things and situations (both positive and negative) – just the way they are, which enables us to enjoy happiness every moment of every day. TYG

The more we love everyone and everything – just

the way they are – the more our cup overflows with happiness. TYG

It is extremely powerful if you can keep on loving everyone and everything every moment of every day, just the way they are, remembering every time you take a breath, so that you maintain a wonderful state of happiness. You may need to love your forgetfulness pretty often, too!

It's true that I had to retrain myself, just as you probably will, to love everyone and everything with loving kindness, just the way they are, but it has now become pretty well automatic for me to do so. The habit builds up the more you do it. Every time I get into a negative state of some sort, I sooner or later remember to love it – just the way it is – and all comes right. I quickly learned that 'sooner' is much better than 'later'.

I now find that it is second nature to love everyone and everything – just the way they are, and I really can say that I am really happy almost all the time. The few times that I am not, I look upon them gratefully as my 'wake-up calls'. If a moment of unhappiness appears in my awareness for any reason, you can guess what I do. I love the unhappiness, with loving kindness, just the way it is, and the love looks after it! TYG

I have also found that the more I practise loving everyone and everything with loving kindness – just the way they are, the more I really cannot stand being unhappy in any way – nor do I need to. TYG

Love–Light

Love and light are really the same thing, and sometimes it is easier to conceive of love in visual terms, as light. Sometimes I call it 'Love–Light' – the love that can be seen shining in deeply loving beings such as Jesus the Christ. If we practise what he said, we find:

- Love–Light will produce a great aura about anyone who regularly radiates love, to all ('that person is an "ever-loving one"'). TYG
- Then anything of a negative nature that comes near the 'ever-loving one' will have its frequency raised automatically by the Love–Light to that of Love. TYG
- In other words, Love–Light will transmute to love the negatives within one's self (fears, desires, pain, rampant and insistent thoughts, etc.). TYG
- There is peace on earth for whoever flows love to all. TYG

Let's Sum up

Everyone can have all the happiness they want, just by loving everyone and everything. It's really simple to do. God made 'loving' just as simple as breathing is, and He gave it to us all.

God our Father–Mother loves us all unconditionally, and gave us the way to pass it on to everyone else, and every thing.

I love God my Father very, very much, and I tell God so every day.

I find it very rewarding in joyous happiness to say several times every day:

Yes, God loves me,

Yes, God loves me,

Yes, God loves me.

The Lord Jesus has told me so, in my heart. And Jesus has told us so in almost every word he spoke.

1 John 3:11

For this is the message that ye heard from the beginning, that we should love one another. TYG

And Lastly

Here are my final words.

Just keep loving everyone and everything, every moment of every day – just the way they are – and you'll be happy.

God bless you!

AFFIRMATION CHANT
I am loving kindness – in action in me now.
I am loving kindness – to God alone, I bow.
I am loving kindness – in mighty cosmic power.
I am the light of God – shining every hour.
I am loving kindness – shining like a sun:
I am God's sacred power – freeing everyone. x3 TYG

Index of Individual Skills and Techniques

A Practice using Frequency · 76
A Sample 'Daily Love List' 110
A Story about Ego · 81
Affirmations · 6, 39, 53, 68, 86, 100
Another Way of Applying Love · 66
Further Ideas to Meditate on · 52
Global Loving · 63
Going up the Ladder · 75
Love All your Negative and Positive Emotions · 100
Love and Light · 35
Love–Light · 121
Love your Humanity as well as your Divinity · 82
Loving Fears · 99
Our Forgiving Nature · 83
Our Thoughts are Where it all Begins · 84
Some of the things Jesus and the Apostles say about Love · 19
The Love Blanket · 65
What we Really Are · 29

Chapters

Chapter 1 · The Logical Mind – or the Heart? · 27
Chapter 2 · What is Love? · 43
Chapter 3 · Methods of Loving · 57
Chapter 4 · Love Your Self · 73
Chapter 5 · Loving Relationships · 93
Chapter 6 · Utilizing the Daily Love List · 105
Chapter 7 · Loving Every Moment · 119
Foreword by Richard Lang · 9

NOTES / LOVE LIST

NOTES/LOVE LIST

If you have enjoyed this book, and particularly if
you are seeking the extra materials offered, please
check out our website,
www.lovingeverymoment.com,
or write with stamped addressed envelope to
Loving Every Moment Books,
c/o Polair Publishing,
P O Box 34886, London w8 6ls

*Polair Publishing's own website is at
www.polairpublishing.co.uk*

*The addresses for the White Eagle Lodge, mentioned in
chapters 3 and 4, and for details of the book* THE LIVING
WORD OF ST JOHN, *is*
New Lands · Brewells Lane
Liss · Hampshire · England
GU33 7HY
www.whiteagle.org